## American Football

If you don't know the difference
between a scrimmage and a huddle,
a chip and a block or a fake and a fumble,
you'll find them all simply and clearly
explained in this book.

If you want to play or watch, all the
information you need is here, updated
especially for the 1986 season.

Eddie Hufford, Director of Physical
Education at the American School in
London, has been an American
Football enthusiast for many years.

# AMERICAN FOOTBALL

**Eddie Hufford**
**Illustrations by Gary Rees**
**Diagrams by Susan Chalk**

KNIGHT BOOKS
Hodder and Stoughton

Copyright © 1984 by Victorama Ltd
Illustrations copyright © 1984 Hodder & Stoughton Ltd
First published by Knight Books 1984
This revised edition published 1986
*Fifth impression 1986*

**British Library C.I.P.**

Hufford, Eddie
  American football.
  1. Football
  I. Title
  796.332     GV951

ISBN 0 340 36194 8

Printed and bound in Great Britain for Hodder and Stoughton
Paperbacks, a division of Hodder and Stoughton Ltd., Mill
Road, Dunton Green, Sevenoaks, Kent (Editorial Office:
47 Bedford Square, London, WC1B 3DP) by Cox & Wyman
Ltd., Reading. Photoset by Rowland Phototypesetting Ltd,
Bury St Edmunds, Suffolk.

# CONTENTS

# INTRODUCTION

American football is traditionally played during the autumn and early winter at professional, college and high-school level. It is a game limited to the North American continent and to American emigrants throughout the world. Though it has its origins in rugby union football, it does have four fundamental differences. It allows the ball to be thrown forward; it allows players not in possession to block other players from the ball; it allows the unlimited substitution in and out of the game from a large squad of players providing there are never more than 11 players from the squad on the field at one time; and it allows the wearing of protective padding and 'armour' by the players.

For the millions of spectators who watch football in stadia across the United States of America and via television throughout the world it is a spectacular form of strategic teamwork.

The object of this book is to outline the basics of the game. You will notice that Imperial measurements are used (they are standard in the USA) but English spellings appear throughout. If in reading this book, you don't understand a word, look it up in the Glossary. That way you'll get to know the technical terms and what they mean, and thus gain a better knowledge of the game.

# ORIGINS AND HISTORY

The Ancient Romans, Greeks and Chinese all played games where a spherical object was kicked or carried. Modern football started as soccer in England and was taken to America by the early colonists. It was played on village greens and on school campuses; the game was strictly local – and very rough.

In 1823 William Webb Ellis at Rugby School in England caught a punted ball, tucked it under his arm, and ran over the end line of the soccer field for the first touchdown in the history of football. This was the beginning of rugby union football.

Rugby developed slowly in England and had not been introduced into the USA when the first inter-collegiate football contest took place on 6 November 1869 at New Brunswick, New Jersey, between the colleges of Rutgers and Princeton. Rutgers beat Princeton 6–4, using Rutgers' rules; the return match was won by Princeton 8–0 a week later, using Princeton's rules. The deciding game was banned by the teachers of both colleges because of the roughness and danger of the games.

Columbia and Yale joined these two colleges in playing football. Harvard eventually learned rugby from a Canadian team and invited delegates from the five colleges to meet in Springfield, Massachusetts, on 23 November 1876 to form a league to play football under rugby union codes. These codes were finally decided on with a special rule to emphasise the touchdown, or try. Yale wanted teams to be composed of only 11 players, which was also agreed. These five colleges formed the basis of the Ivy League – the name given to the inter-collegiate leagues of America's oldest universities.

From these eastern colleges football spread to the American Mid-West in 1879, to the south in 1880, the deep south in 1888 and to the Pacific coast in the early 1890s.

The move away from the rugby union football code began with Yale's 11-a-side ruling, and in 1880 the 'line of scrimmage' was introduced instead of the scrum. This gave possession to one team and allowed the ball to be put back into play from the scrimmage line. Walter Camp, 'the father of American football', in 1882 introduced a rule that required a team to either gain 5 yards in three 'downs' or give possession to the other team.

Teams were divided into seven forwards, or rushers, and four backs. The game was started, following a down, by the centre forward heeling the ball backwards, as in rugby league, to the quarterback, who was not allowed to run with it but had to pass it to either one of the two halfbacks or the fullback. Initially, tackling was not allowed below the waist, but other techniques developed which caused very serious and sometimes fatal injuries. Because of this, President Roosevelt in 1905 threatened to ban the game by presidential edict if the brutality persisted.

In 1906 the National Collegiate Athletic Association (NCAA), along with Walter Camp, set up a rules committee. This committee:
■ legalised the forward pass,
■ created the 'neutral zone' between the teams,
■ required a minimum of six men on the line of scrimmage on offence,
■ raised the yardage for a down from five yards to 10, and
■ marked the field like a chessboard.

In 1910 the committee established further rules which:
■ outlawed the flying tackle,
■ required seven men on the line of scrimmage,
■ outlawed crawling and the flying wedge,
■ allowed a forward pass from anywhere 15 yards behind the line of scrimmage,
■ divided the two halves of the game to make four equal quarters in time,
■ marked the field like a 'gridiron', and
■ allowed the substitution of players in and out of the game.

These rules required some further revision, and the modern game really started in 1912. From time to time changes have been made since then, depending on the developments within the game, to maintain a balance between offence and defence.

# PROFESSIONAL FOOTBALL

Professional football started in 1895 when a YMCA team from Latrobe, Pennsylvania, played for whatever money it could get. Other teams developed, and in 1920 the American Professional Football Association (APFA) was formed, being strengthened in 1922 under the directorship of Joe Carr, who renamed it the National Football League (NFL). It prospered until the Second World War, when its activity waned. Then, in 1945, the All American Football Conference (AAFC) was formed, and by the 1950s a balance had been obtained between the NFL and the AAFC. However, in 1959 the American Football League (AFL) was organised, and the AAFC declined. In 1970 the NFL and AFL merged to form a new NFL with two 'conferences', the National Football Conference and the American Football Conference, each with three divisions, as follows:

## AMERICAN FOOTBALL CONFERENCE (AFC)

| Eastern Division | Central Division | Western Division |
|---|---|---|
| Baltimore Colts | Cincinnati Bengals | Denver Broncos |
| Buffalo Bills | Cleveland Browns | Kansas City Chiefs |
| Miami Dolphins | Houston Oilers | Los Angeles Raiders |
| New England Patriots | Pittsburgh Steelers | San Diego Chargers |
| New York Jets | | Seattle Seahawks |

# NATIONAL FOOTBALL CONFERENCE (NFC)

| Eastern Division | Central Division | Western Division |
|---|---|---|
| Dallas Cowboys | Chicago Bears | Atlanta Falcons |
| New York Giants | Detroit Lions | Los Angeles Rams |
| Philadelphia Eagles | Green Bay Packers | New Orleans Saints |
| St Louis Cardinals | Minnesota Vikings | San Francisco '49s |
| Washington Redskins | Tampa Bay Buccaneers | |

In 1983 the United States Football League (USFL) started as a spring–summer league and is therefore not in direct competition with NFL. The USFL has teams in 12 major American cities.

# COLLEGIATE FOOTBALL

The collegiate football organisation is administered by the National Collegiate Athletic Association (NCAA) or the National Association of Intercollegiate Athletics (NAIA). These organisations set national standards on rules, recruiting, eligibility, and length of season. Most colleges belong to 'conferences' that are made up of similar institutions in terms of size and locations. The major ones are:

## Pacific Ten
Stanford
U.C. (University College) Berkeley
Oregon
Oregon State
U.C.L.A. (University of California, Los Angeles)
U.S.C. (University of Southern California)
Washington
Arizona
Arizona State
Washington State

## Western Athletic
San Diego
Utah
Brigham Young
Hawaii
Texas El Paso
New Mexico
Air Force
Colorado State
Wyoming

## Big Eight
Colorado
Oklahoma
Kansas
Kansas State
Oklahoma State
Nebraska
Missouri
Iowa State

## Big Ten
Minneapolis (Minnesota)
Iowa
Wisconsin
Northwestern
Illinois
Purdue
Indiana
Ohio State
Michigan
Michigan State

## Ivy League

Cornell
Pennsylvania
Princeton
Columbia
Dartmouth
Yale
Brown
Harvard

## South West

Texas Tech
Arkansas
Texas Christian
Southern Methodist
Baylor
Texas
Texas Agricultural &
  Mechanical
Houston
Rice

## South Eastern

Louisiana State
Mississippi
Mississippi State
Alabama
Vanderbilt
Aulsurn
Florida
Kentucky
Tennessee
Georgia

## Pacific Coast Athletic Association

San Jose State
University of the Pacific
Fresno
Long Beach
Fullerton
Utah

## Missouri Valley

New Mexico State
West Texas State
Tulsa
Wichita State
Drake
Illinois
Indiana
Southern Illinois

## Atlantic Coast

Maryland
Virginia
Duke
North Carolina
North Carolina State
Wake Forest
Clemson
Georgia Tech

# BOWL COMPETITIONS

Post-season bowl games, which are now a popular and publicised part of college and professional football, are played in January at the end of the regular season. They began as an afterthought. They derive their name from the silver bowls which are presented as trophies to the winners. The first bowl game was played on 1 January 1902 as an added attraction for the Tournament of Roses in Pasadena, California. The Rose Bowl has been played in Pasadena ever since between the conference winners of the Big Ten and the Pacific Ten (see page 12).

The success of the Rose Bowl led to other post-season games being organised. These are regionally important and sometimes for specific conference winners, or least-beaten teams, and have scouts signing up teams before the end of the season.

The major bowls still current are:
  Sugar Bowl, New Orleans, Louisiana
  Orange Bowl, Miami, Florida
  Cotton Bowl, Dallas, Texas
  Gator Bowl, Jacksonville, Florida
  Sun Bowl, El Paso, Texas
  Bluebonnet Bowl, Houston, Texas
  Tangerine Bowl, Orlando, Florida
  Liberty Bowl, Atlanta, Georgia
  Fiesta Bowl, Tempe, Arizona
  Independence Bowl, Shreveport, Louisiana
  Holiday Bowl, San Diego, California
  Hall of Fame Classic, Birmingham, Alabama
  Aloha Bowl, Hawaii.

The Super Bowl is the post-season game in the Professional League between the winners of the AFC and NFC (see pages 10 and 11). It was first played in 1967 following a suggestion of Lamar Hunt, the owner of the Kansas City Chiefs. The vast audience, both live and via television, make it a tremendous money-maker and a spectacular show.

# BASIC RULES

The game of American football is played with 11 men in each team. The substitution of players in and out of the game allows colleges to carry squads consisting of up to 90 players, although the NFL allows only 45 in professional football.

The winner of the game is the team that at the end of the four quarters of play, in total 60 minutes, has scored the most points.

Points can be scored as follows:

1. **Touchdown**, 6 points. The points are gained either by a player carrying the ball over the goal line into the opposing team's end zone (see Figure 1), or by catching a legal pass in the opposing team's end zone. A touchdown is also allowed if an offensive 'fumble' is recovered in the end zone that had been kicked in by the 'offensive' team and touched down by the 'defensive' team.

2. **Point after touchdown** (PAT), 1 point. After touchdown, one further point is scored, thus 'converting' the six points of touchdown to seven points, for kicking the ball from a play at the line of scrimmage at the two-yard line (in professional, the three-yard line in collegiate) anywhere between the inbound lines (see Figure 1), over the cross bar and between the uprights of the goal (like a conversion in rugby union).

(In collegiate rules 2 points can be earned by running or passing the ball. This option is not possible in professional football.)

3. **Field goal**, 3 points. The ball must be kicked over the cross bar and between the uprights of the goal either from a drop kick or from a place kick at any time during the game.

4. **Safety**, 2 points. These are awarded to the team whose defensive unit tackles an offensive ball carrier behind his own goal line. A safety can also be scored when an offensive player is penalised for an infraction behind the goal line. Lastly, it

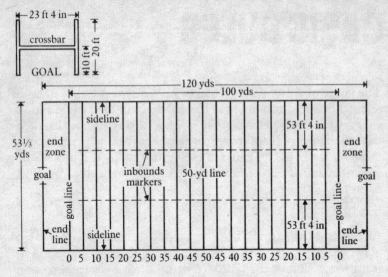

Fig. I: *The regulation college football field and goal. The field can be adjusted slightly for professional, college, or high-school play.*

can be scored if the ball is snapped, carried or fumbled behind the goal line or if a snapped ball hits the goal post. The defensive player of the same name (see Figure 7) has nothing to do with this method of scoring.

The game is played on a rectangular field composed of either natural grass or artificial turf. It is marked in the form of a gridiron, as illustrated in Figure I.

The ball is similar in shape to a rugby ball – a 'prolate spheroid' – and has a leather or composition cover enclosing a rubber bladder. It is between 11 and 11¼ inches long and weighs between 14 and 15 ounces. The professional game uses a brown leather ball, whereas collegiate and high-school football use either a leather or a composition ball with two white bands running around the ball at each end of the laces.

The game starts with a player from one team kicking the ball from a tee on the ground on his own 40-yard line (35-yard line in the professional game) into his opponents' half of the field. His team must be behind him when he kicks the ball. The ball must go 10 yards or be touched by an opposing receiver before the kicking team can touch it. Any player on

Offence        Line of scrimmage        Defence

Fig. 2: *A typical line up prior to the snap.*

the receiving team may catch or pick up the ball and attempt to carry it towards the kicker's goal line. As the ball carrier runs up the field, the opponents try to tackle him to stop his forward movement by getting him to the ground. Where this takes place an imaginary line parallel to the goal line is established; this is known as the line of scrimmage (see Figures 2, 5, 6 and 7).

The team in possession of the ball then puts the ball back into play from within the closest inbound marker on the line of scrimmage, with both teams lined up facing each other (see Figure 2). To do this, the offensive team (the one with the ball) must have seven men on the line when this takes place, although the defensive team (the one without the ball) can be anywhere behind the line of scrimmage. The centre lineman passes the ball between his legs (known as the 'snap') to a back (see Figure 3), usually the quarterback, who either tries to run with it himself, hand it to another back ('handoff') to run with it (see Figure 4), or will attempt to throw it forwards from behind the line of scrimmage to an eligible receiver. The only players eligible to receive this forward pass are any players not

Fig. 3: *The 'snap': the transfer of the ball from the centre to the quarterback.*

Fig. 4: *'Handing off': the quarterback transfers the ball to a running back.*

Line of scrimmage

Fig. 5: *Only the offensive players marked with a circle are eligible to catch passes, although any defensive player may intercept and return a pass.*

on the line at the time of the snap, or one of the two men who are at each end of the line at the time of the snap (see Figure 5).

A running play occurs as the runner's team-mates try to clear a path for him by 'blocking' out the opponents' tackles (see page 46). The runner keeps going until his forward movement is stopped by an opponent's tackle and he is held to the ground by the tackler (see page 48). Where this occurs is known as a 'down' and a new line of scrimmage is established.

A forward pass play occurs when the quarterback tries to throw the ball forward to an eligible receiver, running in a specific pre-arranged pattern (see examples in Figure 22), towards his opponents' goal line. If the receiver catches the ball before it hits the ground he tries to run forward until he is stopped (as in a running play), when a down again occurs and a new line of scrimmage is established.

If the receiver fails to catch the ball or the ball is thrown outside the boundary of the field of play (outside the side- and end lines) the pass is called incomplete and the ball is 'dead'.

The ball is still considered as a down and it is returned to the last line of scrimmage.

Only one forward pass is allowed during each down. A team has to gain 10 yards in four downs. If it fails to do so it must give the ball to the other team at the point where the fourth down occurred.

Usually on the fourth down a team not likely to gain the necessary yards will choose to kick the ball as far as possible into the opponents' half of the field, where it is received and played as in the starting kick-off.

If a team does gain 10 yards in four downs it retains the ball and tries to gain another 10 yards in another four downs.

By successfully and repeatedly covering the 10 yards with each set of four downs, the team not only keeps possession of the ball but also moves downfield towards the opponents' goal.

# NFL, NCAA AND HIGH-SCHOOL RULES

The actual rulebooks for NFL, NCAA and high-school football are very detailed and not many people are conversant with all the rules. (High-school football rules are closest to NCAA, but have considerably more safety factors.) From time to time rule changes take place in order to maintain some balance between the strategic skills of offence and defence. The following is a synopsis of these rules:

On the offensive team all players except one back must be stationary before the snap for at least a second. All backs must be at least one yard behind the line at the time of the snap. No player is allowed into the neutral zone, or is allowed to touch his opponent, prior to the snap.

On the forward pass if the ball is touched by an eligible receiver it can then be caught by any offensive player. All members of the defensive team are allowed to intercept the forward pass and run with it. If a ball is caught simultaneously by an eligible receiver from each team, possession is given to the team that made the pass.

Since the game is one of possession of the ball and the necessity to gain territory, the use of penalties in controlling the game by taking away downs – the same as taking away yards gained – for infringements is very far reaching.

The penalties range from the loss of a down, to the loss of 5 yards, 10 yards and 15 yards of territory or even disqualification from the game. The small yardages are for technical offences, whereas the greater distances are given for rough, unsportsmanlike and unfair behaviour.

The NFL and NCAA have differences in their rules, as follows:

■ The NCAA squads can be of any number up to 90 for home games and often travel with over 60. NFL squads are limited to 45 men. In both cases, the teams consist of 11 men from each squad.

■ The NFL kick-off is from the 35-yard line; NCAA use the 40-yard line.

■ Holding an opponent receives a 10-yard penalty in NCAA, a 15-yard penalty in NFL.

■ The NCAA goal posts are 23 feet 4 inches wide; NFL are 18 feet 6 inches wide.

■ The NFL ball is all leather and is plain; the NCAA ball can be leather, rubber or composition and has two white stripes.

■ NCAA use either five or six officials, whereas NFL use seven.

■ In NCAA rules a fumble can be advanced only by the team that fumbles the ball, whereas an NFL fumble can be picked up by any player from either side.

■ On point after touchdown (PAT), NCAA allow the option of either kicking for one point *or* running/passing the ball back over the end line for two points; NFL allow only a kick for one point.

■ In NCAA a quarterback has to be tackled to the ground for the referee's whistle to be blown, whereas NFL have a quick whistle rule which protects the quarterback by having the whistle stop the game as soon as he is touched.

■ NCAA allow games to end in a tied score, whereas NFL play 'sudden death' overtime of 15 minutes in duration to get a winner.

■ In NCAA rules the kick for the point after touchdown is from the three-yard line; in NFL rules the kick is from the two-yard line.

■ A receiver in NCAA needs to have one foot only in bounds (inside the field) on catching the ball; NFL require two feet to be in bounds.

■ Missed field goal attempts in NCAA are from the 20-yard line, whereas NFL is either from the last line of scrimmage or the 20-yard line, whichever is furthest from the goal line.

■ In NCAA a running back or receiver must stop, and a down must automatically take place, if any part of his body, other than his hands or feet, touches the ground; in NFL he must be tackled for the down to occur.

# PLAYER POSITIONS

## OFFENSIVE TEAM

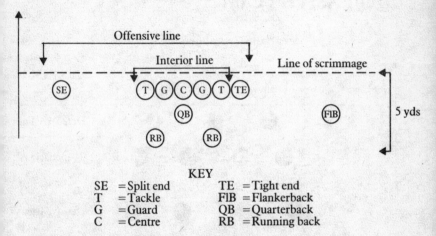

Fig. 6: *The offensive line up at the start of a game.*

SE = Split end. Mainly a receiver of a pass from a quarterback after a scrimmage; he will also have to block for a running back (see page 46).

T = Tackle. The big men who block for the backs and protect the quarterback. In NFL they are normally about 20 stone in weight.

G = Guard. They are usually very agile and are blockers. They are the smallest of the linemen (about 18 stone).

C = Centre. He passes the ball between his legs (the snap) to the quarterback; he is also a blocker.

TE = Tight end. He is both a blocker and can receive a pass from a quarterback after a scrimmage.

FLB = Flankerback. He is a wide receiver, who receives the ball near a sideline rather than centrefield.

QB = Quarterback. He leads the offence by receiving the ball after a snap and calling the strategy of play in the 'huddle';

he is the passer of the ball to the eligible receivers (the SE, TE or the RBs).

RB = Running back. They are the ball carriers in running plays, ball receivers, blockers for other backs, and also fake possession.

# DEFENSIVE TEAM

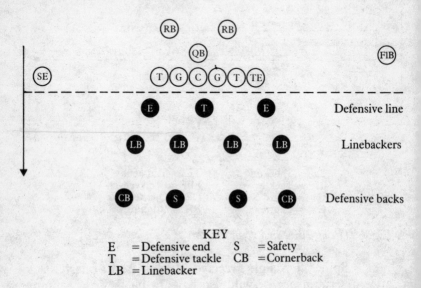

Fig. 7: *The defensive line up at the start of a game.*

CB = Cornerback. They are fast and agile and cover wide receivers.

LB = Line backer. They are the second line of defence who block for ball carriers, pass receivers and sometimes the quarterback. They must be fast and attacking, and in NFL are normally about 17 stone in weight.

E = Defensive end. These are the main attackers of the quarterback and also tacklers (when proximity permits) of ball carriers. In NFL they are normally about 18 stone in weight.

T = Defensive tackle. He is the main attacker of the block in an attempt to stop the play. In NFL he is normally about 19 stone in weight.

s = Safety. They are in the last line of defence, opposite to whichever players are acting as offensive ends.

Since NFL limits squads to 45 players a typical one will consist of:

   8 offensive linemen
   7 defensive linemen
   7 line backers
   7 defensive backs
   4 wide receivers
   3 quarterbacks
   2 tight ends
   1 kicker
   1 punter

The remaining 5 players will be either offensive or defensive linemen depending on the expected strengths and weaknesses of the opposition.

# SHIRT NUMBERS

Because players have certain functions they must wear certain numbers on their shirts for particular positions so that the officials know who are eligible receivers. Players can play other positions with the original number if they inform the officials before play begins.

The following shirt numbers are allowed in NFL:

1–19 quarterbacks, kickers, punters;

20–49 running backs, corner back, safeties;

50–59 centres and linebackers;

60–79 interior linemen (tacklers and guards) and defensive linemen;

80–89 tight ends, split ends and flanker backs;

90–99 defensive linemen (as well as 60–79).

# EQUIPMENT

## THE BALL

This is a 'prolate spheroid' – similar in shape to a rugby ball but more streamlined (see Figure 8). The laces are used to allow the thrower to spiral the ball through the air like a torpedo.

Fig. 8: *The official   ball is made of rawhide and has an eight-lace construction.*

The NCAA and high-school ball has two white bands running around it, whereas the NFL ball is plain brown leather. Sports shops in the USA stock balls of reduced sizes – between three-quarters and seven-eighths of the full size – for younger players.

A top-quality ball will cost between £25 and £30, although plastic or composition balls are available for around £2.

# PLAYERS' EQUIPMENT

## Helmets and face guards

Until the end of the Second World War players wore helmets made of leather – somewhat like Biggles' flying hat. The development of plastics since then has allowed very sophisticated and safer helmets to be produced. They have an outer shell of polycarbonate and an inside of vinyl foam and polystyrene arranged in a honeycomb for both impact resistance and comfort. Many serious and fatal injuries have been caused by players using their helmets as rams or spears (which is illegal); this has resulted in paralysis because of damage to the spinal cord and the neck. Manufacturers now put clear warnings on helmets that they should not be used as rams.

Helmets are held on with chinstraps and have face guards attached. When face guards were first introduced along with plastic helmets, players did not want to wear them. However, various designs have emerged which allow good vision while still protecting the eyes and mouth (see Figure 9).

All players wear mouth guards to protect the teeth and gums.

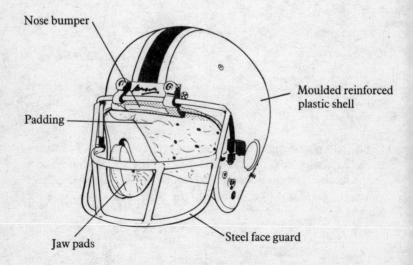

Nose bumper

Moulded reinforced plastic shell

Padding

Jaw pads

Steel face guard

Fig. 9: *A typical protective helmet and face mask.*

A top-quality helmet will cost about £45 and a face guard about £10. It is extremely dangerous to attempt to play the game with cheap, poorly designed helmets and expect any sort of protection.

## Pads and protectors

A fully equipped lineman adds about 13 to 14 pounds in weight when putting on his protective equipment, and even this, following the development of nylon, polyurethane and vinyl padding, is about half the weight it used to be.

The shoulder pads are the most noticeable item which all players wear (see Figure 10). Hip, thigh and knee pads are worn depending on the player's position, and sometimes hip and spine protectors too. A jockstrap with a protective cup (somewhat like a cricketer's) is also worn.

The ankles, wrists, fingers and knees are taped, an essential part of being prepared for football. Teams have 'trainers' whose job is to look after the taping and injury rehabilitation of the team.

Other minor protection is given with the wearing of shin guards, elbow and knee braces, wrist braces and thumb and knuckle protectors.

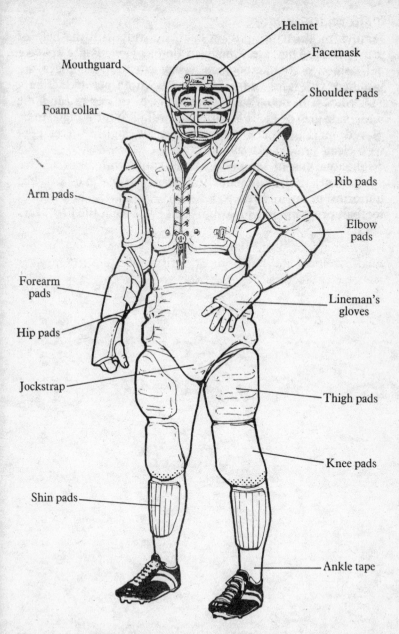

Helmet

Facemask

Mouthguard

Shoulder pads

Foam collar

Rib pads

Arm pads

Elbow pads

Forearm pads

Lineman's gloves

Hip pads

Jockstrap

Thigh pads

Knee pads

Shin pads

Ankle tape

Fig. 10: *A football player's protective equipment. Concealed under his shirt these pads create a rather bizarre sight.*

# Uniforms

**Jerseys or shirts** are put on over the pads with the help of team-mates. They are usually made of nylon. **Pants** are like old-fashioned 'knickerbockers'. They extend to the knees, are fastened with laces and held in place with a belt (see Figure 11). **Shoes or boots** vary tremendously in design, and the underside grip of the sole varies according to the surface to be played on. The most common is like an English soccer boot with cleats (studs) or a moulded sole.

The total cost of equipping an NFL squad with all-protective equipment, uniforms, sideline team wear, and practice uniforms is about £125,000 a year. To start a high-school football programme will cost at least £70,000 in the first year.

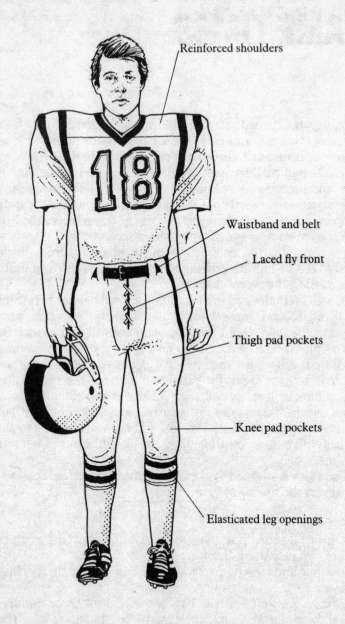

Reinforced shoulders

Waistband and belt

Laced fly front

Thigh pad pockets

Knee pad pockets

Elasticated leg openings

Fig. 11: *A player's shirt and pants need to combine flexibility and durability.*

# GAME TIMES

Although the game is 60 minutes in length, divided into four quarters of 15 minutes each, most games last for about 2½ to 3 hours because the clock is stopped while the ball is not in play. During this 3-hour period the ball is 'live', that is, in play, for about 12 to 15 minutes. An average down where the ball is passed forward to a receiver by the quarterback lasts between 5 and 10 seconds, and an average down where the ball is run forward by a back is only 5 to 7 seconds.

The time for the complete game is made up from 'time outs' plus a 15-minute half-time intermission, and two-minute intermissions between quarters.

In NFL and televised games there are commercial breaks of up to 60 seconds each which do not always coincide with regular time outs. In a normal game there will be between 60 and 75 plays, each of which can take up to the maximum time permitted; this allows the offensive team 25 seconds (NCAA) or 30 seconds (NFL) to put the ball into play (up to the snap). The two-minute drill at the end of each half can also extend a game when the clock does not start following a kick-off until the ball has been touched by a player. The offence usually tries to get as many plays in as possible using passes to the out of bounds sideline.

The clock is stopped by the official timer for various reasons. However, the main ones are:

1. After a score.
2. After an incomplete pass.
3. During a team time out – each team is allowed three per half of two minutes in length.
4. During an infraction of the rules and during the penalty awarded for it.
5. After a kick-off and the ball becomes dead three minutes are allowed for the kicking team to be substituted by the defensive squad and the receiving squad to be substituted by an offensive squad.

6. After a player who is holding the ball goes out of bounds.
7. After the ball is thrown out of bounds.
8. At the referee's request.

# STRATEGY

The strategic aspect of American football cannot be emphasised too much. The coach on the sideline, in conjunction with the quarterback, decides the type of offence to be used. The quarterback then tells the plan of attack to the offensive squad in the 'huddle' and explains the number codes to be used. The numbers and names called out prior to the snap then mean specific duties to specific players, and also tell all the players when the ball is to be snapped. Players have to learn the patterns of play from a book especially put together for their team. They have to memorise them and be able to recall them very quickly and accurately. Figure 12 illustrates a pattern of play.

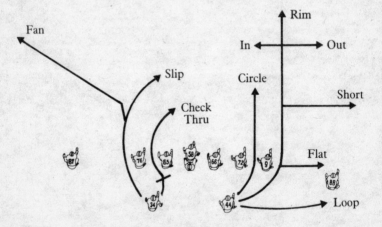

Fig. 12: *Some of the most frequently used pass patterns for running backs. In general, a pattern's name describes its route.*

The offensive line-up illustrated in Figures 2 and 6 is the basic formation. However, teams have various offensive formations which involve players taking up slightly different positions, but not being drastic enough to tell the defence which play is to be used. Only one player on the offensive team is allowed to move prior to the snap (usually the flankerback) and he can run or move only across the field and not towards the defensive team.

Examples of offensive formations are illustrated in Figures 13 to 21.

KEY

| | | | |
|---|---|---|---|
| Q | = Quarterback | FB | = Fullback |
| RB | = Running back | TB | = Tailback |
| SE | = Split end | HB | = Halfback |
| FlB | = Flankerback | WB | = Wingback |
| TE | = Tight end | C | = Centre |
| T | = Tackle | G | = Ground |

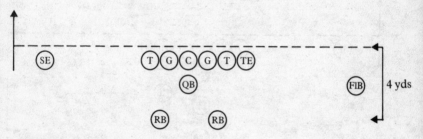

**Offensive Formations**

Fig. 13: *The 'pro set' formation.*

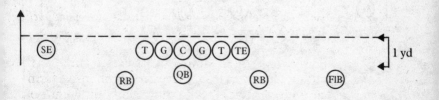

Fig. 14: *The 'spread set' formation.*

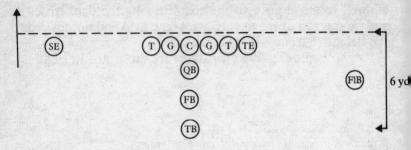

Fig. 15: *The 'I' formation.*

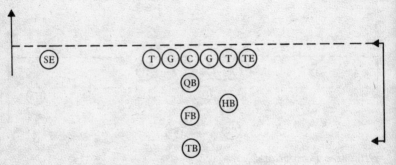

Fig. 16: *The 'power I' formation.*

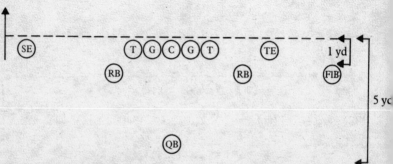

Fig. 17: *The 'shotgun' formation.*

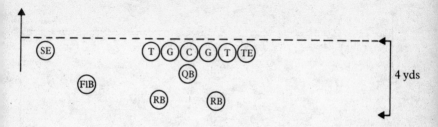

Fig. 18: *The 'slot' or 'twin set' formation.*

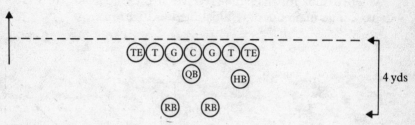

Fig. 19: *The 'short yardage' formation.*

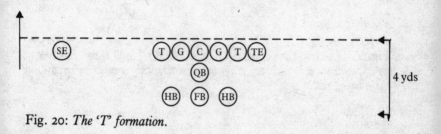

Fig. 20: *The 'T' formation.*

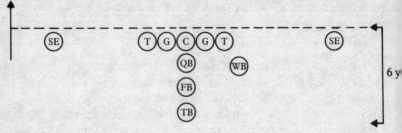

Fig. 21: *The 'I slot' formation.*

6 y

A receiver will run a specific pattern (depending on the quarterback's instructions) so that the quarterback knows where to look for an eligible receiver in order to make a forward pass. The main ones are illustrated in Figure 22.

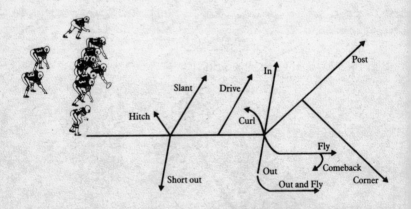

Fig. 22: *The* basic *possible pass patterns for a football team. Because of its appearance when shown diagrammatically, this is often referred to as the passing tree.*

Special teams are used in specific situations – at the kick-off, when converting a touchdown, for a field goal attempt, and when punting:

■ **At the kick-off.** The team that wins the toss at the beginning of the game has the choice of either kicking off or receiving or selecting which goal to defend. Usually a team will choose to receive the kick-off. Once a score has been made the team that has scored then kicks off in turn. The kick-off team will have a squad of fast linebackers and defensive backs who try to keep the ball as well as one specialist kicker who uses a plastic tee to set up the ball for the kick (unlike rugby which uses a mound of turf and a hole dug with the boot).

■ **Conversion of a touchdown.** A specialist kicker will attempt to kick the ball over the goal across the bar. The ball is passed back from the snap, so that a player catches the ball and holds it upright on the ground for the kicker to kick (see Figure 23) before the opposition defensive ends try to charge down the kick.

Fig. 23: *A kicking play: hoping to convert a touchdown, the kicker is aided by a team-mate.*

■ **Field goal attempt**. This is similar to the conversion of a touchdown technique (see page 15). Usually kickers will attempt only distances that are possible for them to kick, since unsuccessful attempts result in the ball being awarded to the opposition for a first down at the point of the snap on the kick.

■ **Punting**. This usually takes place on the fourth down (see page 20) in order to get the ball as far into the opposition's half as possible. The procedure is: from the snap the ball is caught directly by the punter, who quickly kicks the ball as high and as far as possible before being tackled or the kick charged down. The team receiving the punt can do one of three things:

■ catch it and attempt a return run until tackled, or
■ catch it and by raising his arm the player can call for a 'fair catch'; if allowed by the referee he must not be tackled and cannot attempt a return run, because the ball becomes 'dead', or
■ allow the ball to land and not touch it, since the punting team cannot do so either.

In these three situations the game is restarted by a down being awarded where:
■ the tackle occurred, or
■ the 'fair catch' occurred, or
■ the ball comes to rest without being touched.

Teams sometimes fake field goal attempts and punts in order to fool the opposition and thereby gain the necessary yards for the first of the four downs by either a passing play or running play.

Defensive teams try to anticipate the play to be used by the offence and set up a counter-pattern. Basically, this involves the defence either in a man-to-man defence, in which each defensive back is responsible for covering a specific offensive receiver and following him everywhere, or in a zone defence, in which defenders are responsible for covering specific areas of the field and covering any receiver entering that zone. The basic defensive formations are illustrated in Figures 24 to 30.

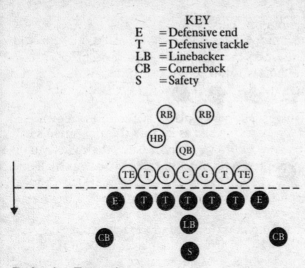

**Defensive Formations**

Fig. 24: *The '7-1-3' formation. In all these examples it can be seen that the figures refer to the number of players in a formation, and their relative positions.*

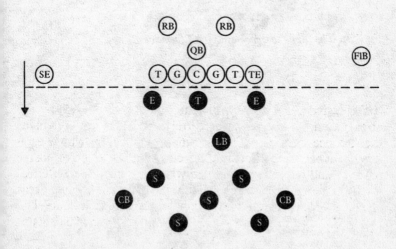

Fig. 25: *The 'penny' defence or '3-1-7' formation.*

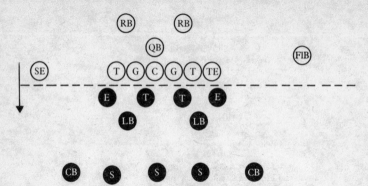

Fig. 26: *The 'nickel' defence or '4-2-5' formation.*

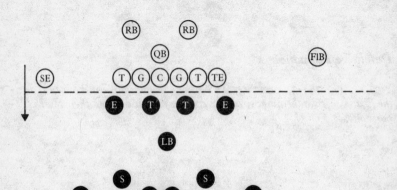

Fig. 27: *The 'dime' defence or '4-1-6' formation.*

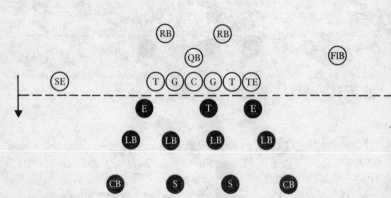

Fig. 28: *The '3-4-4' formation.*

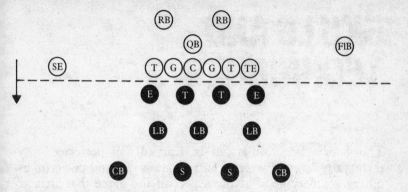

Fig. 29: *The '4-3-4' formation.*

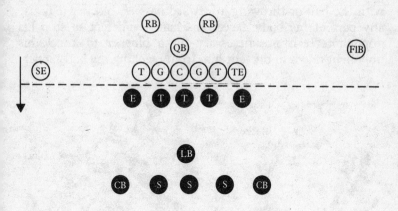

Fig. 30: *The '5-1-5' formation.*

Each squad in a team has a captain, and defensive captains decide the strategy of the defence and tell it to the rest of the squad in the huddle. The captain determines this strategy on the basis of the number of downs, the territory already gained by the offence, and the area of the field the team is in.

# SKILLS AND TECHNIQUES

The game's basic skills can be learned and perfected only through practice. Players who are not as fast and powerful as others get very good at the aspect of the game that attracts them.

## BLOCKING

This is the technique used by an offensive player stopping a defensive player from getting to the ball carrier (see Figure 31). Blocking is essential whether the ball carrier is running with the ball or throwing a forward pass. A blocker may use any part of his body except his hands and feet to stop his opponent. It is not necessary for a blocker to knock his opponent down to prevent him from reaching the ball carrier.

Fig. 31: *Blocking: an offensive player's attempts to floor or deter a potential tackler of the ball-carrier. Here are a shoulder block (left) and a body block (right).*

A shoulder block is the most common for linemen at the scrimmage. The blocker takes up a 'three-point stance' – a crouch position with feet about shoulder width apart, one foot slightly in front of the other with one hand on the ground, knuckles down; the free arm rests against the bent knee. The blocker is now ready to jam his shoulder into the opponent as the centre lineman snaps the ball. If the line moves prior to the snap everyone must be absolutely still for one second before the snap can be done (see page 20). The blocker usually aims at the opponent's stomach area, keeping low and using short, driving steps.

A body block is where the blocker twists sideways just before he hits the opponent. He drops to the ground on making contact and if he hits the thighs he can put the opponent on to the ground. The blocker is not allowed to hit an opponent from behind or he will be penalised for 'clipping' (see Figure 32).

Fig. 32: *Clipping: an illegal block from behind and below the waist.*

Blocking is not just an individual skill. Sometimes two blockers will work together to keep an opponent away from the ball carrier. Occasionally a blocker will run in front of the ball carrier and sacrifice himself, or commit himself to a particular tackle regardless of its possible success, in order for a gap to be found for the ball carrier through the defence.

# TACKLING

Tackling is a technique used by a defensive player using his body and arms to bring a ball carrier to the ground or stop his forward progress (see Figure 33). If the tackle is made from the front, the tackler hits the ball carrier with his shoulder just above the carrier's knees, wraps his arms around the legs, and lifts and drives the ball carrier off balance and on to the ground. If the tackle is from the side, a similar technique is used. However, sometimes only one arm or leg can be grabbed which is often sufficient to get the ball carrier off balance. If a powerful ball carrier needs to be tackled, sometimes two or three defensive players will tackle him simultaneously. The injuries to players occur mostly in tackling (although some derive from blocking).

Fig. 33: *Tackling: any defender may tackle the ball-carrier in an attempt to stop him. The only tackles not permitted are those which involve grasping a player's face mask or tripping with a leg.*

# KICKING

Very few players in the squad are kickers. They are specialists and kick in one of three ways.

## A punt

A team unlikely to make 10 yards in four downs gets the ball as far away from its own goal line on the fourth down by punting – kicking the ball down the field (see Figure 34). Speed is essential, and the ball is snapped directly to the kicker. He catches it about 15 yards behind the line of scrimmage, holds it in two hands in front of him and drops it on to the instep of his kicking foot after taking a couple of steps forward. The ball usually spirals through the air.

Fig. 34: *Punting: a method of kicking used to enable a team to gain distance in exchange for possession.*

## A place kick

Place kicks are used at the kick-off, on a free kick after a safety, or from the line of scrimmage. They can be used on a field goal attempt. The kicker places the ball on a plastic tee in an almost upright position and kicks it with his toe about half way between the centre and the bottom of the ball (see Figure 35). In field goal attempts the ball is positioned on the tee by a team-mate. The kicker usually does not have much of a run-up to the ball.

Fig. 35: *Place kicking: used to score field goals. The ball is set on a tee (for kick-off or a free kick) or set up by another player (for a field goal try).*

## A drop kick

This is identical to a rugby-type drop kick. The kicker drops the ball on to the ground point first and kicks it with the toe just below the centre of the ball as it leaves the ground. The ball usually travels through the air end over end. Drop kicks are not used very often.

# RUNNING WITH THE BALL

Backs or eligible receivers gain yardage by using the technique of running with the ball. The ball carrier protects the ball from being taken by an opponent, or from fumbling, by putting the palm of his hand around the front of the ball and tucking it against his side, keeping it there with his arm and elbow (see Figure 36). The ball is usually tucked under the arm away from potential tacklers, leaving the closer arm for fending off the tacklers. Runners follow their blockers and constantly change direction and pace in an attempt to gain as many yards as possible.

Fig. 36: *Running: the runner holds the ball firmly to his side and protects it with his forearm and elbow as he advances up the field.*

# PASSING

Passing is usually undertaken only by the quarterback, although sometimes the other backs or occasionally the end lineman will throw legally.

A pass must be thrown from behind the line of scrimmage. The ball is held with the fingers of the throwing hand across the laces and the thumb spread behind the laces. The elbow is in front of the body and the ball is brought from behind the ear and released with a snap of the wrist (see Figure 37). The ball usually spirals through the air, which makes it easier to catch.

Fig. 37: *Forward passing: one of football's more difficult but most useful skills.*

# PASS RECEIVING

Only eligible receivers can receive a pass. These are all the defensive players, and the backs and ends on the offensive team. If a defensive player catches a pass it is considered an interception and he can keep possession and attempt to run towards his opponents' goal line. The receivers on the offensive team use speed to run a particular pattern down the field, shake off the defence and be in a position to look for and successfully catch a direct throw from the quarterback. The receiver must keep his eyes on the ball, make a pocket with his hands and when the ball enters the hands bring the ball into his body (see Figure 38). This frequently has to be done while the receiver is moving, looking over his shoulder and trying to avoid the defence. The act of receiving in offence needs considerable practice.

Fig. 38: *Pass receiving: this is done by one of five offensive players eligible to catch a forward pass.*

# PROFESSIONAL FOOTBALLERS AND SALARIES

Players usually start playing football between the ages of 10 and 14 years old at junior high school, with more vigorous, demanding conditioning and strengthening occurring until the end of high school (at 18 years). In order to play inter-collegiate football a player has to be outstanding at his chosen position. College football can be a real money-maker for the total sports programme of the college, and it is normal for football coaches to have a powerful position within the college. The sale of tickets for games, the selling of programmes, and in some cases television coverage can bring in a lot of money. If a college game is televised nationally it is worth over a million dollars to each team, with the Rose Bowl (see page 14) worth over five million dollars.

At the end of a successful college football career the better players turn professional via the 'draft', a system whereby all players graduating and leaving college who wish to play professionally are put on a list. Teams then have training camps where players are invited to participate. The results of these try-outs, as well as the reports of scouts who have watched players throughout the regular season, are used by NFL clubs in choosing players. The team that has finished the season in last position gets first pick of new players, with the champion team getting the last pick. Each team gets 12 choices, always in the same order of picking. Since NFL squads are limited to 45 men, obviously not many college graduates turn professional each year. Professional clubs can also sign players who are free agents, or swap players, or claim players who have been put on waivers by clubs that originally wanted the players but are willing to let them go.

Professional players can earn large sums of money, and also earn bonuses for winning and further fees for endorsing products (using their names in advertisements).

In the early 1980s professional players went on strike for several weeks in order to get better salaries and contracts from the owners of the teams. Each NFL team is owned by businessmen/women who obviously do not want to lose money. The average salary for a professional football player is about $100,000 or £75,000 per year. The better players with other business interests can earn up to £500,000 a year and quite a few players are millionaires. In 1984 in the USFL one player signed a contract for $40 million.

Top coaches of NFL teams earn about £300,000 a year, while top college coaches will get up to about £50,000 a year.

Obviously, television has had a tremendous impact on teams, yet despite wide television coverage seats in the stadia are selling very well at both collegiate and professional level. Modern football grounds will comfortably seat between 50,000 and 80,000 people for professional games. Some of the stadia like the Astrodome in Houston, Texas, and the Silverdome in Pontiac, Michigan, are indoors with artificial grass fields. Most stadia have large television screens so that instant replays can be viewed. Collegiate games have had crowds of well over 100,000.

Football was first televised in 1939, but it was not until the 1960s that it had a real impact on viewing audiences. The coverage is very detailed, with cameras covering every angle, even from a balloon in the air, and with instant replays and analysis. Each year each NFL team gets several million pounds in revenue from television.

Advertising costs to advertisers during the Super Bowls are about £1,000,000 per minute; these television advertisements reach a national audience of over 100,000,000 people.

# INJURIES

The rules of the game have been changed since the beginning of the twentieth century in an effort to cut down violence and the maiming of players. Many of the injuries are to the knee joint, which is very vulnerable, and to the knee ligaments, which if damaged usually require surgery.

The wearing of padding and helmets obviously helps reduce the number of injuries. However, many illegal violent tactics are employed; if these are seen by the officials the guilty team is penalised by the awarding of territory to the team suffering the injury or by sending the offending player off.

The rules of the game allow the ball carrier to be tackled from several directions simultaneously, which can cause very severe injuries. All teams from high school upwards spend a lot of time on conditioning and strengthening players before any games are played.

# OFFICIALS

Fig. 39: *The chain gang: in a dispute over the yardage gained, these officials come on to the field to measure how much of the ball extends beyond or touches the yard marker for a first down.*

The officials who control the game wear striped black and white shirts. There are seven officials in NFL and only six in NCAA; basically they do the same jobs. Experienced officials in NFL earn about £700 per regular game, with £2,500 for the Super Bowl game. The officials are:

**The referee** is in overall charge of the game and interprets the rules. He is positioned behind the scrimmage line (about 12 yards) and watches the quarterback or punter. He signals all fouls.

**The umpire** is responsible for the players' equipment being correct and legal. He is usually five yards behind the line-backers and watches the line of scrimmage and blocking.

**The head linesman** is responsible for watching for encroachment prior to the snap, keeping track of downs and territory gained and lost with the help of the 'chain gang' (see Figure 39) and for the sidelines on his side of the field.

**The line judge** is responsible for the timing of the game (as a double check on the clock operator) and watches eligible receivers and the pass. He is on the opposite side of the field to the head linesman.

**The back judge** watches out for any holding or illegal use of hands by the defence, and is responsible for watching pass interference and the sideline.

**The field judge** is responsible for blocking violations, holding or illegal use of hands, timing the 30 seconds between plays and the intermission and for field goal attempts.

**The side judge** overlaps most of the other judges and is responsible for the various loose ball situations.

A system of signalling all decisions is used (see Figure 40); this is fairly standard. The use of radio microphone allows the decision to be broadcast immediately from the field as well as signalled.

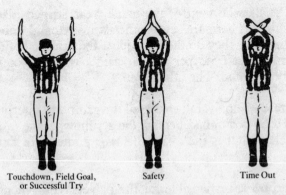

Touchdown, Field Goal,     Safety     Time Out
or Successful Try

Fig. 40: *The official signals.*

Dead Ball or Neutral
Zone Established

First Down

Personal Foul

Ball Illegally Touched,
Kicked, or Batted

Delay of Game

No Time Out or
Time In With Whistle

Offside or Encroaching

Holding

Penalty Refused,
Incomplete Pass, Play
Over, or Missed Field Goal

Illegal Use of Hands,
Arms, or Body

Pass Juggled Inbounds,
Caught Out of Bounds

Illegal Forward Pass

Interference With
Forward Pass
or Fair Catch

Invalid Fair Catch Signal

Loss of Down

Illegal Contact

Illegal Motion at Snap

Crawling, Pushing, or
Helping Runner

Unsportsmanlike Conduct
(Non-contact Fouls)

Tripping

Illegal Crackback

Intentional
Grounding of Pass

Illegal Cut or Blocking
Below the Waist

Touching a Forward Pass
or Scrimmage Kick

Player Disqualified

Ineligible Receiver or
Ineligible Member of
Kicking Team Downfield

False Start, Illegal Shift,
Procedure, or Formation

**Game records statisticians** are employed to record minute details of points scored, yards gained by both passing and running, interceptions made, and kicks made (for examples, see the tables on pages 67–72). Books are published on the details of the major NCAA and NFL teams.

# PERSONALITIES

## PLAYERS

**Samuel Baugh**, a quarterback-place kicker, between 1937 and 1952 introduced the side arm slingshot style of passing-playing.

**George Blanda**, a quarterback-place kicker, played until the age of 48 and between 1949 and 1975 established the record for scoring the most points.

**Jim Brown**, a running back for the Cleveland Browns, between 1957 and 1965 established the record for gaining the most territory.

**Walter Camp**, 'the father of American football', was responsible while still at Yale for reducing the size of teams from 15 to 11 men. He was responsible for picking the first 'All American' team in 1889. In 1906 and 1912 he was a member of the committee that changed the rules of the game to basically what they are today.

**Harold 'Red' Grange** was a nationally known football superstar in the 1920s who was known as the Galloping Ghost while at Illinois University. He turned professional with the Chicago Bears.

**Pudge Heffelfinger** was Yale's 'All American' guard for three consecutive years and was acknowledged as the first professional in 1892.

**O. J. Simpson** was a very fast running back and allegedly the highest-paid player ever in NFL.

**Francis Tarkenton**, known as 'Fran the Scram', is a quarterback who holds the record for completed passes.

**Jim Thorpe**, the 'Touchdown Chief', was an excellent athlete who won gold medals in the 1912 Olympics.

## COACHES

**Paul Bryant** has coached more winning teams than any other college coach.

**George Halas** is known as the 'grandpappy' of football. He coached the Chicago Bears for 40 seasons and was part of professional football when it started in the 1920s. He won more games than any other coach.

**Tom Landry**, the present coach of the Dallas Cowboys, is famous for his ability to win championships and for wearing so-called 'lucky' hats.

**Vince Lombardi**, the coach of the Green Bay Packers and the Washington Redskins, had the Super Bowl trophy named after him.

**Amos Alonzo Stagg** was responsible for inventing the huddle, the centre snap, playbooks (listing the various possible plays), the tackling dummy (or bag) and numbers on shirts.

# AMERICAN FOOTBALL IN THE UK

Until Channel 4 started to broadcast American football games on television in the early 1980s, very little of it was seen in the UK. At the professional level, the first two NFL teams to play in the UK played at Wembley Stadium on 6 August 1983 when Minnesota Vikings played St Louis Cardinals in The Global Cup.

Games are played regularly between September and November on US military bases and at the high schools attached to these bases. The teams are properly equipped and prepared and offer an opportunity to see a live game in the UK. If there's an American military base near where you live, find out if you can watch any of these games.

In the last three years over 200 clubs have developed in the UK, made up of ex patriot Americans as well as British players. Various organizations have emerged in an attempt to both control and promote the game and listed below are the names of teams and organizations currently in existence. The British season varies according to the organization involved, however it is basically a spring/summer season from March until September.

If you are interested in seeing or joining a team, you can make contact either by telephoning your local 'Sports Council' office (number in the telephone directory) or by getting a copy of *Gridiron UK* – a monthly magazine available at newsagents or bookshops, which lists the current teams and who to contact if you are interested. This magazine also gives excellent coverage of the game in the UK as well as in the USA.

## Budweiser League

Ashford Olympians

Basingstoke Cavaliers

Bradford Dolphins

Bristol Bombers

Cardiff Tigers

Chingford Centurions

Colchester Gladiators

Crawley Raiders

Duchy Destroyers

Eastbourne Crusaders

Fulham Cardinals

Greenwich Rams

Havering Saxons

Hereford Chargers

Lee Valley Warriors

Leyland Roadrunners

London Lasers

Mounts Bay Buccaneers

Newtown GWs

Nottingham Cavaliers

Oxford Bulldogs

Plymouth Admirals

Rockingham Rebels

Slough Silverbacks

South Star Scorpions

Southend Sabres

Streatham Olympians

Swinton Sharks

Thames Valley Chargers

Torbay Trojans

Weston Stars

Windsor Monarchs

Wrekin Giants

Basildon Braves

Bournemouth Bobcats

Brighton B52s

Cambridge County Cats

Chelmsford Cherokees

City of London Stags

Collier Row AFC

Croydon Coyotes

Dunstable Cowboys

Farnham Knights

Gloucester Boars

Halton Demons

Heathrow Jets

Huskies AFC

Leeds Cobras

London Capitals

London Ravens

Newcastle Browns

Northampton Stormbringers

Orpington Owls

Pharaohs AFC

Reading Renegades

Royals

South Coast Sharks

Southampton Seahawks

Stockport Falcons

Swindon Steelers

Taunton Wyverns

Thanet Vikings

Washington Presidents

Wight Rhinos

Wolverhampton Outlaws

## British American Football League (B.A.F.L.)

Ayr Burners

Black Country Nailers

Coventry Bears

Ealing Eagles

Birmingham Bulls

Clydesdale Colts

Crewe Railroaders

East Kilbride Pirates

Edinburgh Blue Eagles
Glasgow Diamonds
Ilford Blackhawks
Kings Lynn Patriots
Leicester Panthers
Locomotive Derby
Manchester All Stars
Mansfield Express
Merton Admirals
Musselburgh Magnums
Newmarket Hornets
Norwich Devils
Portsmouth Warriors
Strathclyde Sheriffs
Tyneside Trojans
Wirral Wolves

Fylde Falcons
Glasgow Lions
Johnstone Crusaders
Leeds Cougars
Leigh Razorbacks
Luton Flyers
Manchester Spartans
Medway Mustangs
Milton Keynes Bucks
Newcastle Senators
North Herts Raiders
Nottingham Hoods
Stoke Spitfires
Surrey Thunderbolts
Walsall Titans
Witney Wildcats

## Amateur American Football Conference (A.A.F.C.)

Kingston Liberators
Macclesfield Giants
Newark Vulcans
Runcorn Lynx
St Helens Cardinals
Scunthorpe Steelers
Sherwood Outlaws
Steel City Giants

## Unaffiliated

Andover Cougars
Bilston Steelers
Braintree Scorpions
Burton Bruins
Canvey Oilers
Chertsey Reapers
Cleveland Generals
Darlington Dragons
East Kent Nomads
Edinburgh Emperors
Harrogate Hawks
Horsham Predators

Bath Gladiators
Boston Blitz
Bristol Slavetraders
Camberley Falcons
Charnwood Greys
Cleadon Crusaders
Cornwall Hurricanes
Dublin Celts
Eccles Bullets 303
Fife Falcons
Hinckley Hurricanes
Hull University

Irvine Seagulls
Lakeland Hounds
London Mets
Manchester MPs
Newcastle University
Redhill Rougheads
Salford Knights
Shetland Redeyes
Strathclyde University
Teeside Polytechnic
Thames Pirates
Welling Warriors

Kent Saxons
Leicester Huntsmen
Lothian Chieftains
Margate Mammoths
Peckham Panthers
Rutherglen Ironhogs
Sheffield Three Ds
South Notts Crusaders
Tamworth Trojans
Thames Barriers
Tweedside Outlaws
Wrexham Brewers

**Junior Teams**

Aberdare Apaches
Ashton Alley Cats
Barrow Bandits
Bedford Buccaneers
Bourne Blackfeet
Carnforth Colts
Colchester Tridents
Cradley Heath Cobras
Durham Gilesgate Stars
Edinburgh Hawks
Fife Centurions
Forest Falcons
Harrogate Hawks
Huntingdon Hawks
Ipswich Stallions
Kidderminster Bluejets
Kingston (Hull) Juniors
Luton Junior Flyers
Mansfield Rambos
Mersey Machetes
Muswell Hill Sharks
Newcastle Vikings
Northfield Vikings
N'ham Little Caesars
Oakwood Tornadoes
Ormskirk Ogres

Andover Bear Cubs
Bangor Bullets
Basildon Bloodsuckers
Blisworth Sharks
Burton Blackhawks
Cheshunt Pumas
Corstorphine Cougars
Croxley Green Gamblers
East Lancs Pumas
Ely City Pythons
Fishermead Eagles
Gloucester Meteors
Hightown Stallions
Invicta Colts
Junior Diamonds
Kilmarnock Marauders
London Locusts
Luton VIth Form Scorpions
Mersey Centurions
Monkseaton All Stars
New Forest Gladiators
Newport 99ers
Norwich Juniors
Oakway Juniors
Oldbrook Crickets
Oxford Bullpups

Oxford Chargers
Portsmouth Admirals
Pudsey Parrots
River Lea Bargers
Sandwell Shox
Shirley Razorbacks
Solihull Sharks
Southern Steelers
Streatham Olympian Jnrs
Suicide Express
Swindon Samurai
Thames Valley Juniors
Tyne Hawks
Warrington Panthers
Westside Warriors
Willenhall Destroyers
Worksop Warriors

Pelsall Longhorns
Portsmouth Elves
Rayleigh Turkeys
Saltash Scorpions
Scarborough Tiger Cats
Shorncliffe Juniors
Southampton Seahawks Colts
Stonehouse Braves
Studley Juniors
Surrey Goldspurs
Tenby Titans
Truro Bananas
Upminster Bengals
Weston Point Raiders
Wigston Gunrunners
Worcester Sorcerors
Wyberton Warriors

# FLAG FOOTBALL

Flag football is a game played widely throughout the USA between groups of friends, in schools, in local play areas and in the armed services. Frequently girls and women play, usually on mixed teams. Basically the rules of the game are those of regular football, but tackling the ball carrier is not allowed. Instead, a flag or strip of material, attached by Velcro to a belt on each player's hips, has to be ripped off and thrown to the ground. This indicates where the tackle would have taken place and is therefore the new line of scrimmage for the next down. Frequently, teams agree to allow quarterbacks more time to control the ball from the snap by playing either a one-, two- or three-second rush, which means that the defence cannot cross the line of scrimmage until one, two or three seconds after the offensive centre has snapped the ball.

Helmets, pads and other protective gear are not worn. To play flag football all that is needed is a ball, some flags and the ground to play on. Sometimes even the flags are not used; instead of tackling a player he merely has to be touched (this is known as touch football).

More and more groups are playing flag football in the UK. In London at weekends during the football season, numerous games are set up in parks like Hyde Park and Regent's Park, frequently with ex-patriot Americans joining in and applying their expertise and knowledge of the rules.

# ALL AMERICAN TEAMS

Since Walter Camp, along with Caspar W. Whitney, chose the first All American Team listing in 1889, many 'AA' teams have been selected by various authorities, governing bodies and the press. None of these lists is official, but the selection and listing goes on from year to year. Obviously it is considered a great honour to be selected for an AA team at whatever level.

# HALL OF FAME

The Football Hall of Fame – a museum displaying a variety of football memorabilia – is in Canton, Ohio. Players are not voted in by the football administrators until five years after retiring from playing. Quarterbacks are the most numerous of the 110-plus members voted in.

# FOOTBALL RECORDS

Statistics are kept for all NFL and NCAA games, and books are published containing the records of individuals and teams. Since a player's college career lasts for only four years, the comparison between NFL and NCAA records is not always appropriate; however these tables (based on records established prior to 1983) list some of the more significant factors of the game.

| Most in a game | College | Professional |
| --- | --- | --- |
| **Points scored:** | 43 – Jim Brown, Syracuse vs. Colgate, 1956 (6 TDs, 7 PATs) | 40 – Ernie Nevers, Chicago Cardinals vs. Chicago Bears, 1929 (6 TDs, 4 PATs) |
| **Yards gained rushing:** | 57 – Kent Kitzmann, Minnesota vs. Illinois, 1977 (266 yards) | 275 – Walter Payton, Chicago vs. Minnesota, 1977 |
| | | 273 – O. J. Simpson, Buffalo vs. Detroit, 1976 |
| | | 250 – O. J. Simpson, Buffalo vs. New England, 1973 |
| **Passes completed:** | 43 – Dave Wilson, Illinois vs. Ohio State, 1980 (attempted 69) | 42 – Richard Todd, N.Y. Jets vs. San Francisco, 1980 |
| | 43 – Rich Campbell, California vs. Florida, 1980 (attempted 53) | 38 – Tommy Kramer, Minnesota vs. Cleveland, 1980 |
| | | 37 – George Blanda, Houston vs. Buffalo, 1964 |
| **Field goals:** | 6 – Vince Fusco, Duke vs. Clemson, 1976 (27, 22, 22, 25, 37, 57 yards; 7 attempts) | 7 – Jim Bakken, St Louis vs. Pittsburgh, 1967 |
| | 6 – Frank Nester, West Virginia vs. Villanova, 1972 (29, 32, 35, 30, 29, 23 yards; 7 attempts) | |
| | 6 – Charley Gogolak, Princeton vs. Rutgers, 1965 (52, 39, 27, 41, 37, 27 yards; 6 attempts) | |

73

# Longest in a game

| | College | Professional |
|---|---|---|
| **Field goal:** | 67 – Joe Williams, Wichita State vs. Southern Illinois, 1978<br>67 – Steve Little, Arkansas vs. Texas, 1977<br>67 – Russell Erxleben, Texas vs. Rice, 1977 | 63 – Tom Dempsey, New Orleans vs. Detroit, 1970 |
| **Interception returns:** | 181 – Charles Phillips, USC vs. Iowa, 1974 (2 interceptions) | 102 – Bob Smith, Detroit vs. Chicago Bears, 1949<br>102 – Erich Barnes, N.Y. Giants vs. Dallas Cowboys, 1962<br>102 – Gary Barbaro, Kansas City vs. Seattle, 1977<br>101 – Richie Petitbon, Chicago vs. Los Angeles, 1962<br>101 – Henry Carr, N.Y. Giants vs. Los Angeles, 1966<br>101 – Tony Greene, Buffalo vs. Kansas City, 1976 |

| Most by a team | College | Professional |
|---|---|---|
| Points in a game: | 103 – Wyoming vs. Northern Colorado (0), 1949 (15 TDs, 13 PATs) | 72 – Washington vs. N.Y. Giants, 1966 |
| Points in a season: | 560 – Brigham Young, 1980 (12 games) | 513 – Houston, 1961 |
| Points, both teams, in a game: | 124 – Oklahoma (82) & Colorado (42), 1980 | 113 – Washington (72) vs. N.Y. Giants (41), 1966 |
| Games lost: | 28 – Virginia, 1958–60 <br> 28 – Kansas State, 1945–48 | 26 – Tampa Bay, 1976–77 |

| Most in a career | College | Professional |
|---|---|---|
| **Points scored:** | (4 yrs) 356 – Tony Dorsett, Pittsburgh, 1973–76 (59 TDs, 2 PATs) (3 yrs) 336 – Steve Owens, Oklahoma, 1967–69 (56 TDs) | 2,002 – George Blanda, Chicago Bears, 1949, 1950–58; Baltimore, 1950; Houston, 1960–66; Oakland, 1967–75 (9 TDs, 943 PATs, 335 FGs) |
| **Touchdowns:** | (4 yrs) – 59 Tony Dorsett, Pittsburgh, 1973–76 (55 rushing, 4 pass receptions) 59 – Glenn Davis, Army, 1943–46 (43 rushing, 14 pass receptions, 2 punt returns) | 126 – Jim Brown, Cleveland, 1957–65 (106-R, 20-P) 113 – Lenny Moore, Baltimore, 1956–67 (63-R, 48-P, 2-RET) 105 – Don Hutson, Green Bay, 1935–45 (3-R, 99-R, 3-RET) |
| **Passes completed:** | (4 yrs) 717 – Mark Herrmann, Purdue, 1977–80 (attempted 1,218) (3 yrs) 642 – Chuck Hixson, SMU, 1968–70 (attempted 1,115) | 3,686 – Frank Tarkenton, Minnesota, 1961–66, 1972–78; N.Y. Giants, 1967–71 2,830 – Johnny Unitas, Baltimore, 1956–72; San Diego, 1973 2,469 – John Brodie, San Francisco, 1957–73 |
| **Yards gained rushing:** | (4 yrs) 1,074 – Tony Dorsett, Pittsburgh, 1973–76 (6,082 yards) (3 yrs) 918 – Ed Marinaro, Cornell, 1969–71 (4,715 yards) | 12,312 – Jim Brown, Cleveland, 1957–65 |

# GLOSSARY

**Blocking:** the intentional obstruction of an opposing player from the front without tripping, holding with the hands or hugging him.

**Chain gang:** the officials on the sideline who operate a 10-yard chain to measure accurately any dispute for a first down.

**Clipping:** an illegal block from the rear below the waist.

**Completion:** to catch a forward pass.

**Dead ball:** after the whistle is blown the ball is no longer 'live' to be played.

**Defensive:** name given to team *without* the ball which is trying to prevent the offensive team from scoring.

**Down:** a play from the line of scrimmage. A team is given four downs to gain 10 yards in order to keep possession. If unsuccessful the ball is given to the other side.

**Delay of game:** the quarterback fails to initiate play within the allowed 30 seconds.

**Draft:** the annual NFL selection meeting of college players.

**Encroachment:** making contact with an opposing player before the snap.

**Fake:** an action, usually by the quarterback, pretending to do something in order to confuse the defence.

**Fumble:** the dropping of the ball by a player who had full control of it. It can be either accidental or as the result of a tackle.

**Gridiron field**: this name was originally given to the field because the markings resembled those made by a griddle or grill.

**Handoff**: the transfer of the ball from the quarterback to a running back.

**Hashmarks**: the lines marking the central strip of the field lengthwise. All plays begin inside the marks along the line of scrimmage.

**Huddle**: the grouping of the offence, prior to the down, being told the strategy and code signal for the next play by the quarterback.

**Incompletion**: a forward pass not caught within bounds.

**Ineligible receivers**: offensive players on the line who are not allowed to catch a forward pass; all are interior linemen.

**In motion**: an offensive player, not on the line, who is allowed to run laterally before the snap is in motion.

**Intentional grounding**: a pass deliberately thrown to the ground by the quarterback to avoid being tackled in possession.

**Interior linemen**: five offensive players (two tackles, two guards, one centre) who form the middle of the scrimmage line of seven men.

**Kicking tee**: a plastic device on which to stand the ball prior to kicking.

**Lateral pass**: a pass in a sideways or backwards direction (as in rugby).

**Lineman**: a player on the front line. There must be seven on the offensive line for each down.

**Line of scrimmage**: the imaginary line running through the ball and across the field where the teams line up facing each other.

**Neutral zone**: the 11-inch strip of ground (the length of the football) straddling the line of scrimmage.

**Offensive**: name given to team in *possession* of the ball which is attacking to score.

**Offside**: a lineman who is beyond the line of scrimmage when the ball is snapped is offside.

**Pass interference**: illegal contact made in an attempt to catch or intercept a forward pass.

**Personal foul**: an act of violent contact which is penalised by loss of territory or banishment from the game.

**Rushing play**: running with the ball following a handoff (see Figure 41) or lateral pass.

Fig. 41: *Pitching out: a lateral pass.*

**Sack**: to tackle the quarterback in possession of the ball behind the line of scrimmage (see Figure 42).

Fig. 42: *A quarterback being sacked.*

**Shift**: a movement of offensive players prior to the snap.

**Snap**: the transfer of the ball from the centre to the quarterback.

**Spearing**: the act of diving on to a player, head first, when he is already on the ground.

**Tackling**: the act of bringing down the ball carrier.

**Time out**: the period during which the game clock is stopped either by the officials or the team captain.